Maternal Legacy

A Mother-Daughter Anthology

Edited by
SUSAN L. AGLIETTI

Vintage'45 Press

Orinda, California
1985

Library of Congress Catalog Card Number
85-050065

ISBN 0-9614375-0-2

Printed in the United States of America
by BookMasters of Ashland, Ohio

Cover Design by
Gayle Cornette of Concord, California

Layout and Book Design by
Mendocino Graphics
Fort Bragg, California

Typesetting by
Comp-Type
Fort Bragg, California

This book is dedicated to my mother, Theresa Levy Burke, whose legacy I will individualize and pass on and to my daughter, Rachel, who will one day do the same.

It is dedicated to the memory of my Aunt, Fay Burke, whose gifts are treasured by those who were privileged to know her.

CONTENTS

Beginnings

Ode to my Daughter, *Alana Harris-Rohr* 9

Remembrance

Battered Daughter, *Mary Lee Starkey* 13
History Lessons, *Jocelyn Trigg* 14
This is Unusually Didactic, *Laurel Speer* 19
Throbbing Sunlight, *Linda Foley* 20

Growth

For Marielle, Turning 12, *Marion Cohen* 25
What Will Be, *Joan Rohr Myers* 30

Adaptation

Lastborn, *Margaret Lacey* 33
Rattlesnake, *Nancy Kay Webb* 42
Mom, I Have Something to Tell You,
     N.C. Foster 46
Rehearsing Mother in G-sharp Minor,
     Jean Pearson 47
Transposition, *Mary Ernestine Beam* 48
Lists, *Catherine Scherer* 49
This Has a Lot to Do with Waiting, Mother . . . ,
     Leah Schweitzer 57

CONTENTS

Identity

You are the Child I Might Have Been,
 Nan Sherman *63*
no matter, *Elaine Starkman* *64*
Legacy, *Mindy Kronenberg* *66*
The Children's Table, *Evelyn Sharenov* *67*

Separation

Sudden and Still, *Ruth Daigon* *71*
Memory of Flesh, *Roberta Parry* *73*
The Listener, *Pat Carr* *81*

Continuity

Poem for Mother's Day, *Serena Fusek* *97*
The Madonna Cycle, *Joyce S. Mettleman* *99*
The Unbroken Circle, *Alana Harris-Rohr* *102*

I gratefully acknowledge the unstinting encouragement of my father, Gerald Burke, who paved the way. . .
I thank my husband, Jean-Pierre, and sons, Raphael and Laurent, for being there. . .

beginnings

ODE TO MY DAUGHTER

by *Alana Harris-Rohr*

After you were conceived,
When you were no more than a tiny cell.
A miniature sea anemone
Clinging to your underwater womb.
Even then
I loved you.
As you grew,
You flowed evenly with my time charts.
Waking when I did,
Sleeping when I ceased to stir.
We moved in synchronization—you and I,
From the very beginning.
Rising and falling
With the rhythms of the day.
Crossing dreamy horizons at night.
Making hidden pacts
By some strange, inner language
Within our bodies.
Oblivious
To the world around us.
Later when my world was overturned,
Dreams falling like bloody flames
Upon a blackened thicket of earth.
My pain became yours.
And as I lie broken in a hospital bed
Fighting for my life,
Your battle raged with equal sorrow.
Light years later,
Our struggles fought and won—
We are still held fast
By that same beam of closeness.
Drawn together
By some distant memory
Of a journey we once traveled together

Through both the sun of the day,
And the shadows of night.
Eons from now,
When we are older.
Me — past my prime,
And you in full bloom with womanly ripeness.
We will still flow together
In peaceful rhythms.
Perhaps in different patterns and designs.
Separated by ideas and years.
But never separated in spirit.
For our souls have been cradled together forever
By love,
By memories,
By time,
In the omnipotent hand of God.

ALANA HARRIS-ROHR of Milwaukee, Wisconsin has been a writer for the last 20 years. This poem is dedicated to her daughter, Brenna, born prematurely two days after the author was operated on for ovarian cancer. It tells of tragedy, a struggle through dark shadows and a bright victory for both her daughter and herself. It is a poem of hope and of love.

remembrance

BATTERED DAUGHTER

by Mary Lee Starkey

I know, Mother. I know what the father did. It was in the kitchen wasn't it? How many times did it happen? Once, twice, a dozen, or was it more? Did not the screams of the toddler arouse you? Where was your lion, Mother? Your claws could have ripped the father's flesh and torn the strap from his hand.

Now you are old. I come not to rescue you from your loneliness just as you rescued me not many years ago. You must have much time for memories. Do the screams of the toddler haunt you? Through the fog of time I can see the tipped bucket, milk on the floor, the kitchen pump with the razor strap hanging on it and then. . . There was pain, pain, pain until the heart could hold no more.

The door of my heart closed. I love you not, Mother. For you, I can feel nothing.

Does your pain of loneliness cut and bruise the body? Fear not, Mother. The moment will come when your heart can hold no more.

MARY LEE STARKEY, a homemaker, resides in Alta Loma, California where she divides her time between writing and other personal interests. Her spiritual relationship with the Great Earth Mother healed many of the psychic wounds inflicted during childhood.

HISTORY LESSONS

by Jocelyn Trigg

My son Luke starts first grade next week. Monday morning he will enter the same front gate I did almost twenty years ago. Other days he will walk out the same front door to meet what looks like it might very well be the same school bus here in rural Mississippi. I know how the wet grass will feel like it's licking his toes at the tip of his sandals on the first hot mornings across the yard.

I said I'd never allow all of this, that he would live his life in a different place and way, that history — mine, I mean — would have no chance to repeat itself. But here we are, things not having gone quite the way I planned back when I blamed my unhappinesses on the boredom and backwardness of this country community, and on my parents — especially my mother.

Mother. I am Mother now. And I will be careful about the kinds of things I have thought my mother should have done differently.

First grade: The thing I remember most happened Picture Day. I felt afraid for whatever reason my five-year-old self found. Would Mama come, please? "We'll see; I'll try to make it," she said.

"My mama's coming for when I have my picture made!" I told my teacher first thing that morning. Soon it was time, so we took our butterfly stomachs in our special clothes and followed the teacher down the big hall, across the oily wooden floor, in a line about as straight as those of the letters we were learning to write. My mother! I remembered. Where was she? We stopped at the door to the back of the stage where the photographer waited behind closed curtains. She wasn't at that end of the hall, either. Maybe she was already up on the stage. . .

Our line began the crawl up the few narrow stairs toward the makeshift studio. Until it was my turn, I

14

couldn't tell what was going on, saw only the flash of the light and heard the silly tease of the photographer trying to get one to settle down long enough to snap a picture, the next shy one to look the camera in the eye just once. All of that was an aside: I wanted Mama.

I strained on tiptoe to look across the back of the stage where we would make our path. Surely I would see her soft body propped against the light rising from the window by the opposite stairs. Surely. But no. Another step up. It was almost my turn. Where was she? No, I shook my head and pulled back when the teacher said I was next. "Here, let's comb your hair."

"No, my mama will when she gets here."

"But she's not here; she's not here yet, and it's your turn."

"I wanna wait for my mama; she said she's coming."

Now, no first grade teacher wants her class in tears, forever crying in the yearbook. Sympathy aside, think how it would make her look. She agreed to let me stand aside and wait; maybe she'll get here in time. I waited and watched, waited and watched. But as I look back now at the empty stairs I saw and the window light that would not show me my mother, it was the absence I expected to see, not her presence. Not now. I knew she was not coming. She had said she would, but she wouldn't. I waited, but with less and less resolve and then, last, I was alone. The teacher wiped my eyes, smoothed my hair with her damp hands, pinched the pin curl on my forehead, and turned me toward the photographer's stool. I walked obediently to it and climbed on.

In the picture my mind took that day, I see my teacher standing at the edge of the curtain, the giggly line of girls and boys waiting behind her to go back to class. The photographer started his standard teases about the little boys in the class or some such, but he soon hushed. He looked at her; she nodded. Then he asked me simply to please look at him. I didn't have to smile, but just look up for just a second, would I, please?

So there I am, a slumped and sad face bound forever in the yearbook and shuffled among the pictures stuffed in an old box in my mother's closet through the years. And there first grade is, reduced to memories of the biggest, most painful disappointment I had known to date. My mother had not shown. She had said she would, then she had not.

Or — I had heard her say she would be there. I was an adult before I realized she had not, as a matter of fact, promised any such thing. Her "we'll see" had meant no, not yes. But I had heard what I wanted to hear. In fact, it seemed almost worse that she had not really broken a promise. If she had not been vague and left things open to interpretation, at least I would not have felt set up. I blamed her.

Later, I finally understood that her, "I'll try; we'll see," was avoidance with a purpose. No doubt she thought I would forget her once I got to school. If I tell her no, her mind must have quickly figured, she'll cry and beg and it'll become a big thing. Pass it off and she'll forget about it. She might have even been tempted to actually be at the school as I'd asked, but there was no point. And what would happen if every mother of every child showed up for every school picture? I had to do some things without her now.

That was in the days before Mother took the factory job she kept for years. Then I had to do lots of things without her, and I always hated it. Going to a sitter's days after grade school, then, older, bringing my younger brother and sister home in the afternoons, barking commands the way I thought a mother would, unlocking the big, quiet, aging house that had sat still all day. The cool air waiting behind the door rushed at me, the house seeming to breathe in my face. Like it's slowly waking up, like it's stretching, I thought, as I walked across the front room to the kitchen. The kids lagged behind outside, so the room was still quiet enough for the clicks and snaps of settling to be heard. And of course the clock ticking loudly. I flipped on lights, opened curtains like sleepy eyelids. And hated the laziness, the emptiness.

To work in the kitchen maybe. See how self-sufficient I am; who needs you, Mom? Or to the telephone to talk to the friend I had been with all day, for company, for voices. There are other people; who needs you, Mom?

It wasn't fair and I was angry, I accused, if not with words, and she answered with words that I wouldn't have all those clothes I like to have so many of if she didn't work. I'd rather have her, I felt, at least in retrospect. She probably knew I could only say I didn't care about the clothes, the things, because I had them. I would care loudly enough if I didn't have them, she remembered from her own girlhood growing up poor in New Orleans. She was doing it for me; she defended herself against the guilt I would try to dress her in.

Maybe it was for me. She said it was, believed it. She couldn't have done it for herself, not consciously. It scares me now to think she might have given in to my selfish demands. Her job was the only one she could get with the little education she had. It wasn't much, but she got off in time to be home a half hour after we were in the afternoons. And it had people. It gave her some sense of life beyond that house and, I understand now, was the way she coped.

My mother was of New Orleans, Roman Catholic background, the oldest of four children in a poor family who nevertheless had electricity because they lived in the city and free street dances on weekend nights for entertainment. She met and married a rural Mississippi boy, of Baptist family, and was brought here to live, unwelcome at first. No electricity in those days, she tells the story, still no indoor plumbing. And no music but the Sunday hymns or the men whistling in the garden or with the cattle or chopping wood. Then there were a few years spent traveling, one child, a second with brain damage, and finally I, the little girl she had wanted, was born.

17

When I was still a toddler, the family settled down on the old home place because my brother was having trouble changing schools so much. Dad would go off to work out of town because there's never been any local work, returning Friday evenings with coconut candy for us kids — at least that's the kind I remember best. Mother mothered us and every other child she could find — children whose mothers worked, or foster children. Always moving on, they each took a part of her with them, and that took a toll. The last she found were a brother and sister, hardly a year apart, whose mother had died and whose crippled father couldn't take care of them. They came to live with us and eventually we were allowed to adopt them. Mother had babies again to need her, want her, fill her time, give her a sense of life.

But they, too, began to grow up. Mother hated the house empty, the silence and stillness of the country. She must have often wondered what she was doing there and kept the questions at bay by staying busy with us kids, then with her job. All for us, she said. I am sorry we never let her feel it was okay to admit she worked for her, too.

Mother does not even remember the day of school pictures in the first grade, and although we talked a little at the time about why I didn't smile for my picture, she had no idea it had been so important to me to have her there.

I know now she would have been there if she had known.

JOCELYN TRIGG is managing editor of the *Southern Quarterly: A Journal of the Arts in the South*. Work, travel and family have kept her on the move until the recent return with her two children to her native Mississippi. ''History Lessons'' grew out of finding herself in a different role, a different time, face to face with how fundamentally her relationship with her mother has influenced her own mothering.

THIS IS UNUSUALLY DIDACTIC

by Laurel Speer

For my 13th birthday, Mother wanted to give
a dinner with elaborate menu and school dance
after. Halfway through standing on her feet
all day, I came home sick and Mother said,
Honey, I'm sorry, but I've gone to all this trouble
and gave the party anyway for adults. In retrospect,
I don't want to say, Mother you blew it because
in fact, she'd spent a lot of hours dipping pears
in candied cinnamon, making mustard sauce
from scratch,
rolling a ham loaf and watching the cheese cake
through its cool down, all which is a lot of work.
This wasn't the time to say, Mother, parties
don't matter. Besides, I had a fever and needed
to go to bed. The point is, and this is unusually
didactic for me; so often we don't know, never
put it together, haven't a clue.

LAUREL SPEER of Tucson, Arizona has written nine
poetry books. Her work has recently appeared in *New
Letters, Event, Kansas Quarterly, Slackwater Review*
and *Writers Forum.*

THROBBING SUNLIGHT

by Linda Foley

The three o'clock schoolbell released me into the light of the spring sun. I am new here and isolated from the others who walk in fluttering, gossiping groups. Pretending absorption in my new surroundings, I walk alone.

The spring sun, color of a sliced apple. Shadows from the elms along the street spatter on the sidewalk, peeling doorways, sullen gas pump. The red-haired attendant is whistling through his freckles. Sun touches my neck, bare legs, pushes me along, a warm stream. The western breeze off the ocean is tangy, settles on my tongue and still-white arms.

The air hums. Sunlight tastes like honey. Laziness, insects, expectations. Like a fat, satisfied cat, the street stretches toward the doorsteps. I, too, feel fat and lazy inside and forget that I am lonely.

On my left, the boarded-up laundromat, then, the empty and overgrown lot, a small stretch of wire fencing, part of which hangs mid-air. Garard's Drugstore. Here, the small door to the shop where my mother works. I say I like to surprise her, but I am really looking for reassurance, a warm spot. The door's shellac is cracked, resists my touch. There is one high stair and a miniscule entry. I climb a narrow flight of some twenty steps. Thick funnels of dust dance above me. Deep droning bounces off the staircase walls. The noise deepens near the top and the floor vibrates. Dust climbs into my nostrils.

Inside the large room, dark heads bob up, some women wave, others call hello accented in Spanish. My mother is the only blonde head bent intently over a piece of material. Guided by her nimble fingers, it runs quickly under the pecking needle of the machine. Hers is one of nearly a hundred squatty machines whose noise fills the cavernous room, ominous like a disturbed beehive.

Every stitch counts here. This is piece work. My mother is quick, reliable. She does not realize I am here until I am right by her side.

I put my hand on her back, bend to kiss her cheek. Even though she can't hear me above the din, I say, *"Gruess Gott, Mutti."* She is glad to see me, even though she is rushed. Her lips move in answer to my greeting, *"Gruess Gott, Spatz."* A gray film of dust sits on her hair, her clothes. This mother is different from the one who runs the house.

To her left sits a large canvas receptacle which holds finished pieces. Mounds of finished pieces. This day my mother had been working on zippers and sleeves. Since she has started to work here, clothing in the department stores has taken on a different meaning for me. I want to tell the clerk that the price is too low.

Different women come by, swinging hefty hips. I imagine I see baskets balancing on their heads filled with grapes and bread loaves. But this is America, the footwork is devoid of music.

Some women catch my mother's eye, gesture in the air with swinging arms, roll eyes at me, yellow-flecked brown marbles. Although everybody yells in order to override the steady noise of the machines, I still cannot make out what is being said. I suspect lip reading. Though I have only been here a few moments, my head is pounding. I am too clean. My mother and I were both clean this morning and I was so because of her. At the dinner table tonight, she will be as fresh as I, forgotten the noise, sweat and dust.

Mutti turns from one of the women, looks at me, smiles, nods her head and looks back at the woman. Conspirators, women-mothers conspiring in my favor.

My mother rises and pushes the canvas receptacle toward another area where the pieces will be connected to other pieces and shortly, there will be many other dresses to join the waiting legions on the racks. Someone pushes a broom along the wooden floor. Her sweat and raspy hello reach me at the same time. She says something about my terrific Mamma and "Shee's a nica lady." I agree, embarrassed because everything is so simple. We smile fat toothy smiles at each other. I know my mother helps many of these women with their English and find it amusing. *Mutti* is the only true foreigner here while all the others are native foreigners. Born here, raised in their own particular ghetto. Still, their accents are every bit as real as my mother's and mine. Perhaps some people never yearn to reach out beyond their prescribed and accepted limitations.

I am offered something to drink. An offering to the new, the American generation, steps away from them and their limitations. I smile but feel angry and inadequate. These women shuffle about with apologetic smiles as if their experiences were inconsequential. I have not labored and should be the water bearer instead. I accept the drink graciously; I am well brought-up. My mother and these women are beating the rocks. I wish to take them to another, a softer place. The woman who gave me the drink smiles as if I had given her a gift.

My head throbs from the steady vibrating noise, my eyes smart from the dust, sweat runs down my sides from the thick heat. I feel as though I shall never stop sneezing. Is this the price of liberty, of freedom?

I motion to leave. Someone says, "What a nica girl, so smart. . .like her Mamma. . ." I hear my mother's fragmented response, "daughter. . .real American. . ."

The thundering noise of the machines hounds me down the stairs like a gathering storm. The door closes on the dust. I imagine becoming a real American but all I can think about are heavy, sweaty women guiding pieces of material in the heat of a droning, sweltering room. All I see is dust; all I feel is heavy, throbbing sunlight.

LINDA FOLEY was 14 when she immigrated with her parents and sister from Germany to New York. She currently resides in Moraga, California where she writes, in part, as a way of transmitting her heritage to her children.

growth

FOR MARIELLE, TURNING 12

by Marion Cohen

Elle, the time is nigh
for the death of childhood
and the birth of childhood memories.

So far, unconceived, they cling to your dark.
Unconceived, unborn. . .but oh! so alive!
and soon, soon to pigeon-perch, to slither
to separate, to find the air
to rise, to spread
to rest on trees
to turn into geese and divide land from sky
to turn into seagulls and divide land from sea
to turn into crows and fill the dome with
    geodesics
to turn into ravens and utter Nevermore.

Elle, I'm afraid of your childhood memories.
I'm afraid of what they'll be.
I'm afraid they'll be those mornings you wake up
    at 11:00 but way before me
all those mornings you finally hear my footsteps
    only to realize they're not coming down but going
    still further up
all those mornings I finally land only to murmur
    hurriedly "Just-a-second-I'll-hug-you-in-a-
    second-just-as-soon-as-I-lay-down-these-poems"
all those mornings I go out to buy the ingredients be-
    fore making breakfast
all those mornings I go out twice because I forget
    the butter
all those mornings the eggs come out the con-
    sistency of daisy centers

all those mornings *you* make breakfast
all those mornings I get mad anyway.

Elle, I'm afraid of your memories.
I'm afraid they'll be those glances I keep
    sneaking at the mailbox
    when you sometimes exclaim "Mommy, there are
    three big envelopes for you, and the
    addresses are in *your* handwriting"
and I don't laugh and hug you.
I'm afraid they'll be *this* morning, the morning
    of your party. I'm not doing the kitchen
    floor like I said I would
but in bed, still, and awake
and in bed I stay, with this poem, with
    this story
in bed I stay, writing, like Cassandra, all
    the sad endings.
And the even-worse things, the things I don't
    think about, the things all *these* things
    are a mere camouflage for, the things I'm
    not arming myself for, the things I can't
    beat you to the punch about.
Oh, I know everybody's human but
I'm taking that into account and
Elle, I'm afraid.
I'm afraid of what you'll remember.

And I'm afraid of what you'll forget.
I'm afraid you'll remember the punishment
    and forget the deed.
I'm afraid you'll remember the noes and
    forget the yeses.
I'm afraid you'll remember that Nancy Drew
    we never finished and forget all the
    ones we did.

I'm afraid you'll remember the death of your
    sister more than the births of your brothers.
I'm afraid you'll forget all the week-long
    birthdays.
I'm afraid you'll forget the great job I did
    on your real, original birth-day.
And I'm afraid you'll remember me screaming, "I
    won't give up writing. I *won't* give up thrift-
    shopping. I gave up math and piano but I *won't*
    give up writing and thrift-shopping."
I'm afraid you'll remember that and forget that
    I also screamed "I *won't* give up my children."

And Elle, I'm scared stiff of your diary.
(Omigod, what'll you write in your diary?)
It's gonna say — I just know it — all about how
    Daddy's sick and Mommy's yelling
Or Mommy's sick and Daddy's yelling.
And the rejection letters, and the rejection words,
    and the peeling car. . .
Oh, El, I'm so afraid by the time we get rich
    and famous, you won't be a kid any more.
I'm so afraid by the time I'm no longer forced to
    say "Sorry kids but I hafta make supper",
    you'll no longer be asking "Will you come in
    the living room and play cards?"
Oh, El, I'm petrified by the time Daddy's
    in shape for running through the fields,
    you'll no longer want to.
I'm terrified by the time we have your child-
    hood just right, it'll be written up (in
    your diary) already.

And your poems — O Elle, don't write too
    many poems!
In particular don't write "Daughter of Culture"

poems or ''Mad Mood Mommy'' poems
And don't get carried away with metaphors, or
    make your extended metaphors too extensive
And make it clear, please, what's a metaphor
    and what isn't.
As for dreams. . .well, Freud says we dream
    our past wishes and
I'm afraid of what you'll dream.
Afraid of what you wish.

Which brings me to your shrink — I'm
    es*pec*ially nervous about *her*.
Maybe she'll say I was too permissive.
Maybe she'll say I was too strict.
Maybe she'll be kind and remind you, from
    time to time, not to blame me, that it's
    really *my* mother's fault.
Maybe she'll warn you, though, to nonetheless
    watch out or you'll turn out like me.
Or maybe (horror of horrors!) maybe
    she'll say I wasn't so great at your
    birth either.

And your true love — What'll you tell
    your true love?
What'll you tell your true love — that you
    never told anyone else?
Will you tell your true love that I don't
    understand you?

I'm not too concerned about your children
Nor your grandchildren.
(By then, I figure, you'll have passed the point
    I am now, and realized.)
But your great-grandchildren, and great-great-

    grandchildren
And your old age, that second childhood. . .
And your deathbed — I'm positively *ter*rified
    of your deathbed.
What faint gurglings will the crowd decipher,
    what secrets will you too late divulge?
I managed your birth-bed fine (At least I think.)
    but what can I do about the ol' deathbed?
I probably won't even be around to edit whatever
    proclamations you make, and if I am, there
    won't be time and it won't be appropriate.
Oh El, what will you say on your deathbed?
What will you say after your deathbed?
"I am preparing," I once wrote
"for my mother's ghost."
And I was
And I did
But *your* ghost, El, is a real toughie
And your ghost, El, is drawing nigh.

Though she's a full-time poet, **DR. MARION COHEN**'s Ph. D. is in math. She teaches Math Anxiety and Poetry workshops at Temple University in Philadelphia, Pennsylvania and also loves classical music, thrift-shopping, feminism and mothering. "For Marielle, Turning 12" is one of her many poems about *motherguilt* in this society.

WHAT WILL BE

[for Rachel]

by Joan Rohr Myers

Now moods will flow
in monthly tides
that downward pull
your longings
for creation
and the universe
into days that are
counted. Know even the moon
that tugs on your life
is held to a pattern,
one circle of possibilities
that whispers to women,
"Even as you feel
life pour from your body
you also will feel
your heart fill
like a teacup."

JOAN ROHR MYERS lives and teaches in Eau Claire, Wisconsin. Her poems have appeared in 100 magazines and anthologies. Three of her plays have been produced and broadcast by the Wisconsin Public Radio network.

adaptation

LASTBORN

by Margaret Lacey

They had never really meant to have three children, but when Liane came along six years after the youngest of her two easy-going brothers they learned to rejoice in a daughter, in a child of their maturity. And as Dana was not aware that they behaved any differently toward Liane than toward the boys, it came as a cruel shock to discover slowly that this daughter of mellowness and experience seemed to have a quarrel with life from the day of her birth.

Her brothers had handled it all with relative grace: learning to share their toys, facing injustice in the classroom, coping with bullies and sibling rivalry. Alex had declined the role of heavy father and had stayed in the background when he could; Dana thought they had met the adolescent crises well: Steven's passion for cars, Daniel's tendency to use his fists in an argument.

Liane was another matter. Easily the most physically beautiful of the children, she was prickly from the start. She was not good at ''mingling''; nursery school meant two years of tearful goodbyes and dozens of solemn conversations with teachers. (''Slow to socialize,'' they told Dana.) All through the first month of kindergarten Liane crouched under her desk with her head in her arms and her bottom presented to the rest of the class. And she had a way of strolling in from first grade at nine A.M., having escaped the eye of the playground monitor.

Dana, who had gone back to an interest in writing after Liane began full days, found that she was either escorting a sullen child back to school, or listening from her upstairs office for the sound of small feet. She and Alex had to remain constantly alert in a way which they had not with the boys. There was no time of day which was safe from a phone call announcing a new crisis; the switchboard at college had standing instructions to track

Alex down if Liane's principal called during the hours when Dana had to be out. Since she never developed any defenses against the worry, the writing did not go well. She began to despair of succeeding at it while Liane lived in the house.

Liane did not grow out of it. Her sharp edges cost her friend after friend; her loneliness turned her sour. She was unwilling, or unable, to do consistently well in classes. "There's nothing wrong with her mind," the school psychologist assured them. "Give her time." Dana gave her time; sometimes it seemed that she also gave her blood, or even that Liane required her mother's soul.

It was not bad enough to keep her out of school. "She is not ill," the psychologist said bluntly. "She is unhappy." Life at home was just bearable with the help of a lot of tripartite homework sessions, and long evenings when Liane sat on one lap or another, simply decompressing.

"They laugh at me. They make fun of my clothes. They tease me about grades. I can't play the games; they won't let me try." She suffered from horrendous bouts of bitterness and rage which she could not express toward their proper targets: the tormenters among her peers. So her family tried to absorb the storms. Dana grew intensely weary of the cliches that followed Liane home from school, but they continued to apply: "chip on her shoulder, low self-image, her own worst enemy."

For a time she had a group: four girls who ate and endured the indignities of the playground together afterwards. But one year their number went to five with the addition of a newcomer. It soon became evident to Dana that the internal dynamics of the group were changing. One awful day she heard the storm door shatter with the force of its closing and hurried down to find her daughter rigid on the couch. The new girl had simply set out to exclude her, and in doing so had caused the fickle affections of the others to shift. That day Liane told Dana: "Melissa said to me: 'You're dumb and ugly and we don't want you around any more. Don't ever sit at our table again.' The others let her do it. They wouldn't look at me. So I went away.''

Dana had to gather the small body into her arms by main force. They sat for two hours before she could be sure she had won the child back to her.

She wanted to kill the vicious, complacent little beasts, or at the very least to inflict pain that would reactivate each time they contemplated another cruelty. She would go to the principal; she would visit home room and make a speech of such eloquence that the children would never forget it. She would sit in all the classes for all the days that were necessary.

"No you won't", Alex said. "You're not going to do any of that. Don't you remember what happened to the kids whose mothers came in to complain?"

She did. Those "protected" children, the ones whose parents had fought their battles for them, had lost ground rather than gaining it. Dana remembered that she too had teased one or two of the weaker ones; thinking of it now she felt shame for the child she had been. She saw herself among her school playmates, ranged like an endless incline of chickens, each turning to inflict hurt upon the one below.

"I was dreadfully lonely," she told Alex. "I went whole years without one good friend. It felt as if I had to fight my way out of school nearly every day."

He nodded. "Me too. And it killed us, right? We both died of loneliness and persecution."

"Well, of course not. We were strong."

She had the grace to laugh when she caught his kindly ironic gaze upon her.

"And you think she's different?"

Dana thought about it all. After a while she said: "It's just not true, is it?"

"What's not true?"

"That childhood is the happiest time of your life."

He stretched his legs as far as they could reach across the floor and clasped his hands behind his head.

"My love, I wouldn't live through those years from ten to twenty again, not for any consideration I can think of."

She said wonderingly: "We've been duped. All those years. Why do they keep saying it? Why do we believe it?"

"Who ever believed it?" he said, and got up to go to bed.

In the spring of her seventh grade year Liane came home with a midterm F in Math. Nothing would comfort her, and she would not, could not, get the hang of it. The after-dinner sessions at the table got more and more stormy. Liane often went to bed in tears; so did her mother, though Dana worked at keeping her own at bay until she could hide them from all but Alex.

She showed him the location of the hurt in her body. "It sits — right here. Not in my head. Right here."

One night, late in the spring, she had a dream. In it she bore the pain as she had the three babies; she could feel its downward progress, like labor, and then she pushed; the pain became a being separate from herself. Still dreaming, she sent it out to earn its fortune.

She told Alex about it in the morning. He looked at her for a time. Then he said: "Do it."

Startled, she asked: "Do what?"

"Bear the pain. And I don't mean hold onto it; I mean birth it. Then send it away."

She stared at him. "But I can't. I have to keep it. She needs me to keep it. That's what mothers are for."

He shook his head. "No. She's thirteen. Your own pain is enough. Let Liane take charge of hers."

She clasped her arms around her middle; she was overcome by a baffling anger.

"But Alex, that's — corrupt. I can't. She won't be able to carry it all."

"Yes, she can."

She was not convinced.

"Look," he said patiently. "If you could cut the pain in half by taking it on, that would be another matter. This way, all you do is double it."

She could not deny it. "But you can't mean it — just give it up?"

He nodded solemnly. But he warned: "It'll take time."

She resisted, she tried to put it out of her mind, but she was not successful. Finally, without telling him, she began timidly to try it. She pictured herself counting sorrows out into neat piles: this pain and that, Dana's, Liane's, Liane's, Dana's, Liane's, Liane's, Liane's. No, it was never going to be any good; Liane's pile kept getting unmanageably large. So she sometimes cheated; she relabelled some of them and hid them in the bottom of her own pile. The difference was that now she knew they were there, separate, discrete, indigestible.

And indeed, there was change. When she took account of herself, she began to imagine that her midsection actually felt lighter.

Liane had a congenial cousin visiting for part of the summer; Dana found that their strife troubled her less than before. When Liane would fly to her room with her feelings hurt, Dana stopped seeking her out for one of those intense private sessions of the past. Alex came through splendidly when there was disciplining to be done, and Liane had always been quicker to forgive when the hard words came from her father.

Summer had tended to be a little easier for Dana in spite of that small grim figure around the house; she somehow imagined the pain of loneliness to be less ferocious than that of ostracism. One or two of the faithless friends came around when they were at loose ends; Dana ground her teeth and let them in. At these times of companionship Liane acquired a radiance that was like a sun-drenched lawn after rain. There was more definition to her, and clarity, as if an obscuring curtain had been drawn aside. She seemed, at those times, to have no memory of past hurt, no consciousness of what was to come. Dana was heartened — and appalled. She ached to warn her daughter, to temper the pleasure with reason, but she always thought better of it.

Liane seemed no worse after such a day, but Dana noticed that she never returned the visits by seeking out the old playmates in their own homes, or if she did, she never spoke about it to her parents. She had always been simply "out" on days when they knew she had been gone from the street.

Late in August Dana found the fragments of three of the second-best china cups behind the piano in the basement. She perceived them to represent a symbolic act.

"You needed to throw them, I suppose?" she asked, more bemused than upset.

Liane said: "I was so angry."

"Could you come and talk to me next time, before you throw things?"

Liane said promptly: "Throw first, talk later."

Dana laughed aloud, and evoked a reluctant grin from Liane; they lived on that grin for days.

But she could not help dreading the opening of school, for she knew that Liane would walk out the door every morning ready, even willing, to be offended. All the old enemies would be waiting for her, and some new ones. Alex offered to be home for her on the first day, since his Monday afternoon was free from classes.

"No," Dana told him. "This one's mine." She made sure she saved some important typing; when Liane crashed through the door at 3:10 she was noisily clattering keys.

"Hello, darling. Welcome home," she called cheerfully. There was no answer. At this point a year ago she would have left her work and gone to find Liane as a vessel ready to be filled to the brim with the day's sorrows, the day's angers. This time she made herself keep working. As the minutes passed the pages became a jungle of errors, but she did not stop to correct them. It was better for the rhythm not to falter.

At last she heard steps on the stairs. Liane came into the room and flung herself on the bed, not speaking.

Dana asked, "What teachers did you get?" and held her breath.

Liane burst out: "Nobody good. The worst teachers in the school. I don't know anybody in my classes. I'm going to hate it. It's worse than last year."

The bile-bitter lump expanded in Dana's chest; she thought it might suffocate her. It wasn't going to work; there was no way she could escape it. But she made herself say quietly: "How do you know you're going to hate it?"

Her daughter gave several frustrated kicks to the counterpane. "Just because it's awful. Because nobody likes me and I don't like anybody. You don't understand. You never did understand."

It was time. And it was going to be her hardest task: harder than sex-education or Math homework, harder than Steven's night in jail or Daniel's broken nose after his worst fight.

"Liane, I'm going to tell you what eighth grade was like for me. I suppose I've never talked about it because I didn't want to make it worse for you. But I see there's no sense in worrying about that now, because you're about as unhappy as you can get. Well, I hated it; I wanted to die. I hated myself and all the teachers, and all my classmates. Nobody ever came home with me after school because nobody liked me. I used to get stomach aches and headaches, and I used to wake up early so I could cry from six to seven in the morning, because if I was lucky that meant I wouldn't have to cry during the day. I got over it, but only because the year went by, and the next year I could go to the high school."

By now she thought she had Liane's attention. There was a listening quality about the one ear she could see.

"The point is," she went on, "I'm really quite a happy person now. I think it's much better to be a grownup than a child or a teenager. I wish you could be a grownup right now, but you can't."

Liane pushed her face still deeper into the bedspread; Dana wondered how she managed to breathe. At least she had not rushed away and slammed her door.

Dana said: "I love you very much, Liane. I'm pretty sure I'll be here as long as you need me. But I can't do eighth grade for you, or age thirteen. I couldn't do any of your other years for you either, and I made a big mistake when I tried."

She waited.

"You know those BEFORE and AFTER pictures in the magazines? Well, your father and I are really supposed to be AFTER. Something to shoot for." She thought she detected a kind of snort, well muffled by fabric; she wondered if it could be laughter. She went on: "We don't always do very well, because it's hard work being an AFTER. To tell you the truth, I've got all I can handle this year, doing forty-three, so what I'm asking is if you would do thirteen by yourself."

Then she put out her hand and just touched a slim ankle; it did not flinch away. "Go get a snack."

After a while Liane pulled herself up from the bed, still silent. Dana did not watch her go, but she heard the door of her room close very quietly. And then she resumed her typing, but the tears blinded her and ran down her nose, so she had to stop and find a Kleenex. She was not able to tell whether she had made any difference, either to herself or her daughter.

Liane did not look at her when she came downstairs. The evening was a subdued one; Liane ate her supper and did her Monday dishes in silence. Somehow Dana sensed that there was no sullenness in her. They watched M*A*S*H together. When Liane got up to go to bed she kissed them both, for the first time in months.

When they went to bed at eleven Liane's door was open an inch or so, and her reading light was still on. Dana hesitated, then went in. "Darling, you should be asleep."

Liane did not appear to have been reading. "I waited for you," she said, and there was a new friendliness in her voice. Dana reflected that raising children played havoc with all the internal organs: now her heart turned over. The narrow face before her, framed by dark, shining hair, was suddenly so beautiful, so intelligent, so *knowing*.

"I really will—I'll try to do thirteen." Liane said. And Dana found herself clasped in a fierce hug, an educated, grown-up hug. "See you in the morning, Mom."

She kept Alex awake for a while, talking about it, but he did not seem to mind. As she was dropping off to sleep he nudged her.

"I was wondering," he said. "since you don't have to do thirteen, could I possibly subcontract forty-six to you?"

MARGARET LACEY was brought up on an Iowa Quaker farm; about half her stories reflect that life. She's also had two psychological thrillers published in *Ellery Queen*, a science fiction piece in the *Christian Science Monitor* and a ghost story in *Mississippi Valley Review*. She's about to begin writing a third mystery novel; the first two are currently out seeking a publisher.

RATTLESNAKE

by Nancy Kay Webb

Last Saturday afternoon my shower was interrupted by Letty, my 9 year old daughter, who told me there was a big rattlesnake under the peach tree. So while she kept an eye on it, I finished my shower, including a second shampoo and a three minute protein conditioning. I was in no particular hurry.

As soon as I was dressed I loaded the 22 with bird shot — I always use bird shot instead of a bullet because shot splays out over a broader area and helps make up for my poor marksmanship. Then I brought the rifle and two extra cartridges outside with me.

Oh, boy, was he a big one, stretched out in the shade under my peach tree. He was the biggest rattlesnake I'd seen since we moved into the Santa Monica mountains.

I shot him once in about the middle of his thick, charcoal colored body — I was aiming for his head — and he began moving, trying to take cover in the tall weeds close by, so I quickly loaded the 22 again and shot, this time at a fairly close range. He did not go any farther, but he continued to move. I had the third cartridge in my pocket.

"Shall I shoot him again, Letty?"

She watched him awhile. Rattlesnakes sometimes go on writhing for half an hour or so after they have been thoroughly dispatched.

"No, Mamma. I think he's had enough."

After a few minutes he turned with his ventral side up, and Letty squatted down beside him.

"Don't get too near," I warned her. "He's still moving."

She inspected the second wound I had made. The shot had gone through him and made a red hole in his belly like a slice a little broader toward one end.

"It looks like a vagina," she told me.

Then we went inside for some tea and muffins with nectarine jam.

"I don't get it, Mother," said Letty.

"What don't you get?"

"It says here, 'Retell as fiction an incident in which you and someone close to you took part. When you finish, read the account to that other person and note how your account changes what really happened.'"

"Yes?"

"So, Mother, nothing like this snake thing ever happened."

"But, Letty, last Saturday..."

"Last Saturday? Last Saturday? Mother, first of all I'm not 9 years old. I'm nearly 18. But that's irrelevant. The important thing is that there wasn't any rattlesnake! There was a tarantula, a smallish tarantula. And *I* was the one taking a shower when you burst in: 'Oh, Letty, Letty there's a tarantula under the peach tree.' I said, 'You deal with it, Mother,' and you said — now correct me if I misquote — you said, 'But, Letty, you know I have arachniphobia.'"

"Well, the assignment says 'retell as *fiction*.' I was making fiction."

"But it isn't interesting fiction. To someone who's not scared of snakes it's very boring fiction. You only think it's interesting because you're terrified of snakes."

"Oh, dear," I said. I felt very unhappy. "Well, I was honest about my shooting, wasn't I? About being a lousy shot?"

"Don't feel bad, Mother. A lot of people are scared of snakes. And don't think it's because you're a woman, either. It has nothing to do with being a woman. Daddy was even more afraid of snakes than you are. I remember once when we heard one rattle he sent you tramping around in the weeds with his army boots on and your nightgown hiked up around your waist — to 'flush it out' he said — and he stood about two hundred yards away with the 22. Yeah, Daddy was a lot more afraid of snakes than you are — but then he was a better shot, too."

"So you think I should write something else for my class?"

"What I really think is that you should give up trying to write and go back to whoring."

"Whoring?"

"Well, what do you call it?"

"I've never called it anything, but if I had to, I guess I'd call it exercising my sexual freedom."

"Okay. Whatever. . .I just think it's a little late in life for you to be picking up something new."

"Letty?"

"What?"

"I'm sure we'll see one around here soon. A snake, I mean. They say the mountains are crawling with them this spring."

I feel terrible. Suppose she's right. . .Suppose she's right. . .I feel so terrible that I can't stand myself. All morning I've tried to coax myself into better spirits. First, I tried daytime t.v.: There was little Phil, drowned in his bath, but restored to life by supplications to Jesus Christ. The testimony of little Phil's father made me cry. So I turned to the news. A retrospective on Haight-Ashbury. That made me cry, too. Then I made my way through all my stand-by remedies: Figs and cream, a sexy book, sitting in the sun to watch the mountains go silver with blooming sage. I even tried something I had never tried before: I trimmed my pubic hair with the sewing scissors...I am becoming more downhearted by the minute. Suppose she's right?

Okay. Right about what? About the writing or about the snakes?

I don't know. Right about either. Right about both. Suppose all of them are right.

All of them?

Yes, all of them. Letty and all the other 18 year olds. My writing class is crawling with them. "You're gettin'

44

it, mamma, you're gettin' it." "Oh, you got something natural going. Just stick with the natural. Don't worry too much about using your brain." The little twerps. I want to start reciting Rimbaud in French, or jerk out my pencil and derive the quadratic equation. The little twerps. Cocky, self-certain little twerps. When I was 18 I figured I would have to wait until I was 2 1/2 times 18 before I was certain. Now I'm 2 1/2 times 18 plus X. And I'm still waiting.

Last night I dreamed about being bitten by a rattlesnake. My husband and I were cutting tall, yellow weeds with our machetes when we came upon him, the young rattler with his beautiful brown and tan diamonds and his beautiful triangular head. The first time he struck he bit my husband, and then he bit me. I woke up scared and I told my husband the dream. He said, "Don't fret, honey. If he bit me first there wasn't much venom left for you." But, of course, I was still dreaming because my husband has been dead for years. So I have to wake up again, and either keep the dream to myself or tell it to Letty, who, probably, will say, "Your dream style, Mother, is of as poor a quality as your prose style. Why don't you stick to material you know something about?"

NANCY KAY WEBB was born in Fort Worth, Texas and received a B.A. in English Literature from Columbia University. Her work has been published in several small press publications around the country. Recently she moved with her husband and three of her four children from Southern California to a farm in Northern California where, along with many other occupations, she continues to write.

MOM, I HAVE SOMETHING TO TELL YOU

by N. C. Foster

"Mom, I have something to tell you.
I'm a Lesbian. I want you to know."
　　Visions of prejudice and fear tumble over my head.
"Mom, I'm in love. I've never been happier."
　　Almost daily I have prayed for her happiness.
"I've known in my heart, for many years, that I was different."
　　Different yes, tom-boy yes, but Lesbian?
"I love you, Mom, and don't want you to worry about me."
　　How often, "Don't worry, Mom," has tugged on my heart.
"You know how I've searched for loyal friends. I've found them."
　　Recalling her loneliness in high school, I sigh.
"Now that you know, please don't tell my brother and sisters."
　　A heavy burden, not to be shared with close family.
"I need time to come out to other people. Mom, I'm scared."
　　I find my voice at last, "Don't be frightened, my
　　daughter. My love will support you always."

N.C. FOSTER is a grandmother living with her retired
husband in Sonoma County, California. She spends her
time writing, sewing and gardening.

REHEARSING MOTHER IN G-SHARP MINOR

by Jean Pearson

The chords come from her,
nerves taut as catgut.
Her hands still play on my life,
blessing and damning with every stroke.
Capriccios of woe take flight,
wrung from my small violin,
exercised since childhood on
guilt, frustration, rages,
pain without words.
Break, heart, into a dark
quartet, your stored German anguish
flushed from the lacquered wood.
Compel the whole world
to weep through you.
Such breaking, she taught you,
is all for your good.

JEAN PEARSON's poetry has appeared in *Mickle Street Review, Blueline, Sparks of Fire: Blake in a New Age* and the *Christian Science Monitor* and is forthcoming in *Earth's Daughters*. A translator of German and Swedish poetry, Jean Pearson is a member of the Feminist Writers' Guild and a contributing editor to the *Mickle Street Review*. Her home is in Bethlehem, Pennsylvania.

TRANSPOSITION

by Mary Ernestine Beam

We meet anew over a hand of cards,
our first since you left,
head held high, and trembling.

The riffling, small slappings of the cards
bring back early games,
rules bent to appease your tiny fierce temper.

With newly acquired urbanity,
you deal a different hand,
spell out rules learned elsewhere.

Under your guidance my score mounts,
then glimpsing your smile, I know —
you are giving me the game.

MARY ERNESTINE BEAM lives with her husband in LaRue County, Kentucky, teaches remedial reading and has two college-aged children. She has published *Homefolks*, a poetry collection, and is presently finalizing publication of two more volumes. She has been writing poetry for four years.

LISTS

by Catherine Scherer

I. Things My Mother Does
That Will One Day Drive Me Crazy

Embarrasses me in public.
Calls me "Chicken Pie".
Delights in saying four-letter words, especially "shit."
Takes ill-gotten gains from the candy displays in stores.
Asks, "Do you want a piece of candy?"
I virtuous, "I never eat ill-gotten gains."
Knows I will accept a piece of candy once we are safely
    out of the store.
Tells the parents of obnoxious brats they have "cute"
    children.
Tells dogwalkers they have "cute" dogs.
Tells them "I like them that size" no matter what size
    they are.
Tells anybody cutting his grass, watering his lawn,
    bullying his grass, "You take such good care of your
    place, it always looks so nice."
Tells them this even though I haven't cut our grass in
    two months.
Tells waitresses, busboys, other customers, but especi-
    ally me, "I worked as a waitress once, in
    Hollywood."
Says this not just once, not just twice.
Says, "All the movie stars used to eat in there, Charlie
    Chaplin, Mae West."
Says, "Charlie Chaplain once asked me for a date. Of
    course, I refused."
Says, "This place" anyplace "reminds me of the place I
    used to work in, in Hollywood."
Asks, "Should I get up and see if the lights are off in the
    bedroom?"
Gets up.
Comes back.

Asks, "Should I get up and see if the lights are off in the
   bedroom?"
Comes back and says, "Go and see if the lights are off in
   the bedroom, I may have turned them on when I was
   just in there."
Yells to me in the kitchen, "You're not putting anything
   on the stove, are you?"
Comes out to check if the stove is turned off.
Comes out to check again, with her hands clasped behind
   her back.
Says, when we are back in the living room, "Go and see
   if the stove is off, I may have turned it on."
Comes out to check after I have checked.
Comes back and says, "Go and see if the stove is off, I
   was just out there and I may have accidentally
   turned it on."
Makes me unsure, is the stove off? Are the lights off?
Makes me think I smell gas, maybe I hear water running.
Maybe
"Did we bring only one shopping bag?"
Constantly interrupts me.
*"Didn't we have two shopping bags? Did we leave one
   behind?"*
Adds her anxieties to mine.
Resists all my attempts
*"Did we have only two umbrellas? Did I wear a hat? I
   didn't*
to add my anxieties to hers.
forget it somewhere, did I?"
Is not impressed that the imminent perils I fear
*"Didn't we leave something behind? Shall I go back and
   check?"*
are indeed imminently perilous.
Goes back to check where we have been sitting to
see if "we" left anything behind.
Asks, "We didn't leave anything behind, did we?"
Says "we" when she means "you".
Says, "Put the dishes away, the cat might eat them."
The cat has gotten fat on crockery and rattles when he

walks. He is ruining his teeth and his digestion. He
is imperiling my mental health.

Sings while walking down the street.

Sings "Old Black Joe" while walking down the street.

Sings, "Where do we go from here, boys,
       Where do we go from here?
       Around the corner to the saloon
       To get a glass of beer."

Thinks up nonsense words I wish I had thought of.

Has secret jokes that I suspect are about me.

Practices sarcasm.

Says, when I say, "I don't know," I don't know if it will
rain, I don't know where she left her glasses, I don't
know who that lady she was just talking to was,

Says, "I thought you knew everything."

Says, "But you went to college."

Says, about the Senator, any senator, "I knew him when
he was a boy selling cookies door to door."

Says about the ex-Governor, any ex-governor, "I knew
him when he was too lazy to walk up a single flight
of stairs, but had to wait for the elevator."

Says about the President, any president, any senator any
ex-governor, and anyone from the state of
Pennsylvania, "His mother used to say, 'He'll never
amount to anything', and now look at him."

What is the moral of this? I can never be sure.

Is it, "Mothers don't always know."

More likely it is, "You can fool everyone else, but you
can't fool your mother."

I know she is practicing sarcasm.

She is driving me crazy because I can never be sure.

Impresses everyone as a sweet, bewildered but cheerful
little old lady.

Disguises herself as the archetypical Little Old Lady. It is
her day to day reality. Perhaps it is even true. The
trouble is, my head has one "little old lady" while
tangled up inside the rest of me is my mother.

And I can never be sure which

II. Movies My Mother Might Have Appeared In While In Hollywood
(an alphabetical listing)

Abbott and Costello Meet Mother
The Amazing Exploits of the Clutching Mother
Anatomy of a Mother
Birth of an Old Lady
Bulldog Old Lady
Confessions of an Old Lady
The Curse of the Old Lady
Danger, Mother at Work
The Daughter Eater
The Devil is a Mother
Dial M for Mother
Dr. Motherlove
Five Mothers to Cairo
Gunga Old Lady (retitled Old Lady Din)
Hail the Conquering Old Lady
Hell Roarin' Old Lady
I Was an Old Lady for the FBI
Lawless Old Lady
Legion of Old Ladies
The Maltese Mother
Mother at Midnight
The Mother Behind the Mask
The Mother Cometh
Mother Comes Home to Roost
The Mother Conspiracy
The Mother in Half Moon Street
Mother Made Me
Mother on the Orient Express
Mother on the Prowl
The Mother Mob
The Mother Who Came to Dinner
The Mother Who Knew Too Much
The Mother With the Golden Arm
My Pal, Mother
The Old Ladies Are Always With Us

The Old Ladies Karamazov
Old Ladies With Dirty Faces
Old Lady Avenger
The Old Lady Blows at Midnight
The Old Lady Came C.O.D.
Old Lady, Jr.
The Old Lady Meets Hollywood
Old Lady Notorious
The Old Lady of Dr. Caligari
Old Lady of the Sierra Madre
Old Lady on the Outlaw Trail
The Old Lady Reforms
The Old Lady Rides with the Boy Scouts
The Old Lady Vanishes
Only Old Ladies Have Wings
Our Old Lady in Havana
The Phantom Old Lady
Phone Call from an Old Lady
The Private Life of an Old Lady
Public Old Lady #1
Reign of the Old Lady
The Return of the Old Lady
Saddle Leather Old Lady
Scarface Old Lady
See Here, Old Lady
Some Old Ladies Are Dangerous
Strategic Mother Command
Ten Mothers to Hell
Thirty Mothers Over Tokyo
This Mother is Mine
Tin-Horned Old Lady
Twenty Thousand Years with an Old Lady
Under Mother's Spell
Up the Old Lady
Where the Old Lady Roams
While Mother Slept
The Wrath of the Old Lady
Yodeling Old Lady from Pine Ridge
You Can't Get Away from Mother

III. More Things My Mother Does That Will One Day Drive Me Crazy

Trusts everyone.
Makes me distrust everyone: are they trying to
    take advantage of a befuddled old lady?
Refuses to make decisions.
Defers to me in everything.
Makes me doubt every decision I make.
Refuses to tell salespeople who call on the phone
    "We're not interested."
Listens to their sales pitch, four minutes, five
    minutes.
Tells them, when they are finally out of breath,
    "You'll have to talk to my daughter, she makes all
    the decisions."
Is afraid of being abandoned.
Especially on buses.
"You won't get off the bus without me, will you?"
Especially
"Don't get off without me."
in restaurants.
"You won't go until I'm finished eating, will you?"
Is afraid I'll finish eating before she finishes.
Has devised ways to make sure I don't finish first.
e.g., by shoving her food onto my plate
"Here, take some of my French Fries."
when
"Here, you eat this peach."
I don't want it.
"Have a piece of my toast."
e.g., by keeping me busy answering questions.
*"Are you going to take me walking when we get out of
    here?"*
"We're not going straight home, are we?"
"You're not in a hurry, are you?"
"You're not going anywhere special, are you?"
"We're going walking, aren't we?"
"Where are we going to walk to?"

e.g., by refusing to eat anymore after I have
    finished eating,
    even though
"I don't want anymore."
"You've hardly eaten anything."
"I just can't eat anymore."
"I'm paying for this, and you're going to waste it!"
"But I've had enough."
"It's good for you, it'll put hair on your chest."
"I don't know if you'll wait for me."
"I'm waiting."
"I'll just finish my fruit, if you're sure you'll wait."
"I'm waiting."
e.g., by threatening to get lost, even though
"Wait for me, I don't know the way home."
"We only live a block from here."
"I'm all turned around. Where do we live, what is my
    address again? What is my last name?"
Makes it difficult for me to disengage my mind
    from her.
Is trying to bind me to her eternally.
Says, always says, always, "You'll take me with you
when you go, won't you."
When she finally drives me crazy, she will no doubt
insist on having an adjoining room in the asylum.

Is sometimes afraid of me.
Makes me feel I am terrorizing an old lady.
Makes me feel like a bully.
Makes me feel I am becoming my father.
The two things my father always said: "Grab the bull
    by the horns," and "Your mother needs a lot of
    looking after."
When my father was in the hospital for the last time,
    he said to me, "Look after your mother, she needs a
    lot of looking after."
I resisted. Men feel they must condescend to the
    frailty of women, of wives, could be of daughters.

If my father exempted me from the frailty of women,
   it's because he mistook me for a man. My father
   perhaps protected my mother's brain into peaceful
   slumber. I refuse to do likewise.
My mother says, "When I worked, I had to be alert,
   but my brain's retired now."
Says, when I say, "Do you ever hear from it?"
Says, "Yes, I just got a nice letter from Florida."
Perhaps my father knew her better than I do.
She is the rock breaking the resolve of the waves.
The weak overpowering the strong.
The meek inheriting the earth.
She is making me something other than I want to be.
She is making me look after her.
Who will look after me?
She is making me be adult all the time, so she can
   play child.
She is the frailty of women, the fragility of old
   age. It frightens me.
Other people go insane in public and melodramatic
   ways. Not to be a bother I am going insane quietly,
   pinprick by pinprick. And when I have gone there,
   everyone will say it's a sad commentary on the
   weakness of my character. They will say I went
   insane from the inside out, because they won't see
   the pinholes.
Says, when I say, "You are going to drive me crazy,
   lady."
Says, "Yes, I really will."
She is practicing sarcasm.
Maybe she is plotting against me.
I am not paranoid. I do not have a persecution complex.
She is driving me crazy because I can never be sure.
But why is she so damn happy about it?

CATHERINE SCHERER is a native of Chicago who
returned to that city six years ago, after the death of her
father, and has resumed life with her mother.

56

THIS HAS A LOT TO DO WITH WAITING, MOTHER...

by Leah Schweitzer

From within the confines of the old house, you spend your days and nights boxed in, unable to get out. I don't know how you do it, but you do. You wait for us to call, and for your friends to visit...you wait to feel better, for the cortisone to numb you out of your frail, arthritic body...you wait for your sister to phone, and for your grandchildren to breakfast with you on Sundays. You wait for letters and for bills — your entire life, it seems, is tightly wrapped in waiting.

I, too, am waiting: for you to have one good day...for you to forget yourself and smile, or laugh at jokes, or run around the block...oh, Mother, why do I expect to see you running around the block? Because I like the idea — I like to see it in my mind's eye, where anything and everything is possible...

I can see you in your twenties: brown-eyed and beautiful, waiting to be delivered from wartime death that's all around you...an immigrant from Rozana, Poland arriving with one of your brothers. . .living in Toronto...meeting that dark and dashing, fascinating anarchist fifteen years your senior, accepting his proposal that arrived in letters from California...following him to Los Angeles...getting married. And more waiting: you wait for him to change his mind about children...you wait for your children to be born...for World War II to be over...for the letters full of horror to stop coming. You wait for us to grow up...you wait for me to have the operation that is supposed to save my life yet leave me lifeless inside...you wait for me to adjust to this...I wait for you to adjust to this...you wait. . .and I wait...

I call to say I'm coming over, and I offer to make lunch. You say you'll wait. How different your voice sounds when you forget yourself — transformed, and full of energy. The violin sadness is gone and you sound, somehow, like another person.

As I drive to the house, I wait. I don't mind this wait because lately something about being in the old, cracking house makes me uneasy. It's only because of you I go there. And when I'm there, I feel the reality of your aging, and of mine, and I feel frightened.

I pull up and gaze at the house for a moment, at how it sits behind the colorless lawn. The red walkway, with its splitting pavement, seems to want to jump out at me. I stand in the little courtyard that's overgrown with weeds, yet seems so proud because it boasts a brilliant and abundant lemon tree that bears such perfect fruit in the surroundings of a lot of imperfection.

I open the door that you keep unlocked most of the day (in spite of our pleading that times are not safe), and I stand in the octagonal entry hall, on what was once a gleaming parquet floor. I glance down at the inlaid pattern of chestnut and honey beige, now dulled, and my eyes pick up the grain in each square, still visible. I look across to the full-length chimes, or chime (what *did* happen to the other one, I wonder), and suddenly I hear their deep, rich vibrations. . .twenty-five years back. . .

A cold shudder runs through me. How much time, I ask myself, how much precious time do we have to be friends, to be close, to fight, to yell, to be angry, to comfort. . .how much time to go through your "pictorial diaries" full of old photos, letters, yellowed clippings and scraps of writing. . .

I'm at your side now. I run my hands along your soft, lined face that looks pink and cherubic and a little puffy today. I touch your hair that looks so snowy and electric — as if it could fly off on its own. We kiss. I look into your hazel eyes, clear and alert, and I see happiness in them.

You ask me to adjust your walker, which you've finally agreed to use, and which is probably too low, because you tell me that you're bending too far over when you use it. As I tighten the screws, I happen to look up. I notice the hunch in your back, more pronounced than ever. And I see that you've set the table. China. And Sabbath candles. "So what else do I have to do?" you ask. And when I open the refrigerator to discover that you've already prepared the lunch — a lovely-looking tuna salad and a jello mold — I hear you say, "I did it while I waited for you." I catch the smile on your face. It means so much to you that you can still do some things for yourself. . .

I bring food to the table, including leftovers from your meals-on-wheels delivery. We eat and have coffee. We talk, about your doctor, who today is such a good-for-nothing, but who just last week was a good man, a *mensch* for making the house call. . .you tell me about your friend Shoshana's birthday lunch, which your friends helped you put on in the house, just so you could be included. . .you tell me you need slippers, and a nightgown, and pajamas — the same items I'm always searching out for you, but that never seem to be just what you had in mind. . .

It's almost time for me to leave. I ask, "What did you want to be when you were a young girl growing up?"

"Wait," you say. "Wait. . .I'll tell you about that the next time you are here."

I wonder if there's a *b'racha*, a prayer, for those who wait.

This has a lot to do with waiting, Mother. . .and I love you.

LEAH SCHWEITZER is a Los Angeles writer, poet, teacher, editor and writing consultant whose work has appeared in such publications as *Crosscurrents, Broomstick, The Literary Monitor, Womanspirit* and the *California State Poetry Quarterly.* Currently she is co-editing a poetry anthology about Israel. She wrote "This Has a Lot to Do with Waiting, Mother. . ." after a specific visit to her mother who had been waging a ten year battle against debilitative rheumatoid arthritis. It speaks of the frustration in not being able to take away pain from a loved one.

identity

YOU ARE THE CHILD I MIGHT HAVE BEEN

by Nan Sherman

Perched on a high cliff
you capture rainbows
for your child to hold.
Through a narrow canyon
you guide strangers,
friends, to warm their fingers
at your open hearth.
Recklessly, you pour life
through a sieved spoon,
spending all gold nuggets,
empty even hidden pockets.
Flowers nod in recognition
open at your touch.
When you laugh
tight faces smile, surprised.
Your soft hands
smooth away pain,
forgiving eyes absolve.
Woman   daughter

You are the mother
I wish I had
the mother I wish
I'd been.
You are the daughter
I want.

You are love.

NAN SHERMAN is a staff consultant at the Women's
Center in Los Angeles. She began writing in 1981 and
has had 30 poems published to date.

no matter

[for Ruthie at 21]

by Elaine Starkman

we're alike
no matter how you hate that fact
or swear we're not

no matter that you were
raised in California sun
and I in a Chicago flat

that you fit
smoothly into your skin
while I struggle with mine

even though you've mastered
feats I'd never dreamt of
at your age
            horses, skiing
            above all your
            magnificent art

even though you hate modern poetry
love the classics and
prefer men for friends

still I know your need
to create your kingdom
purer than my own has become

I know too well
your fear of breathing
in my house

your fear of attack
by family rulers
of being strangled by me

your need to slam
the door and make me
watch from the outside

yes, how alike we are

ELAINE STARKMAN is a San Francisco Bay Area
writer. Her "Letter to Naomi" appears in *Between
Ourselves — Letters Between Mothers & Daughters*
(Houghton Mifflin, 1983). She is editor of two
anthologies of women's poems on peace and teaches
English at Diablo Valley College in Pleasant Hill,
California.

LEGACY

by Mindy Kronenberg

In the mirror
heredity grins, it cracks
at the mouth
clutches at the corners
of my eyes.

Is it me in her
or her in me?

We don't discuss it.
She gets older,
I mature,
and we move like one dancer
in a time-worn mirror.

My laughter is hers
but the jokes are my own,
as are my hands
& what I do with them.

Traitor that I am,
I collect her silences
& put them into words,
creating poems instead of children.

Will she forgive
my dark sense of humor,
these wicked fingers
that hammer her life?

Try as I might
to enclose myself in silence,
I hear heredity titter
& taunt me with her laughter.

MINDY H. KRONENBERG is a poet, writer and free
lance editor living on Long Island.

THE CHILDREN'S TABLE

by Evelyn Sharenov

A part of my side, like Creation,
    a daughter —
Separated on holidays by a long table,
    lit candles, a roast,
She sat flanked by noisy cousins at
    the children's table.

We have become each other — daughter,
    mother —
Revolving in the night as one,
    lightly felt as
Familiar strangers knocking shyly at
    the warm windows of our own house.

A curtain is pulled aside. I recognize
    my smiling gracious daughter.
She presides, generous, passing
    a platter.
Her hair, like mine, grays into its brown
    like the watered-down wine

That filled her glass at
    the children's table.
It is a single moment, swiftly spent
    carrying the whiff of death
That comes with
    prescience.

Knowing the next season before
    it arrives
And is briefly exposed before settling
    buried by the season to come
We move up a generation, like
    layers of time.

Before clearing the dishes I sit heavily,
    one last time in the bridge chair
My daughter's chair, still warm after years.
    Like billiards the family has gone home
To their pockets and the children's table is folded
    and returned to the closet.

EVELYN SHARENOV's fiction and poetry have appeared in several literary magazines and she is currently
at work on a novel. A native New Yorker, she presently
resides in Southern California with her husband and
family.

separation

SUDDEN AND STILL

[to Betsy]

by Ruth Daigon

Here to my hiding place, stranger,
bring me a cube, a sphere, a cylinder
to fill the empty spaces;
lizards, wild flowers, shallots,
to soften a stone tongue of land;
wine, fire opal, ripening grain,
to make me fertile again.

You slept so light,
hardly an imprint on the sheets
to witness you were there.
Now, your presence, an eyelash
caught in a tear duct —
even after your death
I keep blinking you back.

Again it's 4 A.M.
last night's wine stain
still on the table cloth,
moonlight coloring in
the shades of sleep.
Again the doorbell rings.
I filter the air
before swallowing.

Which child is it?

Then I catch a breath for my dead girl,
hold it in my mouth
until the house is stilled
and I as motionless as she.

How long will you keep my hand
cooling in yours?

I hold you cubed in my palm,
turn my wrist to see
the infant, child, woman,
and reach through you
to find myself.

Asleep, your father hunts
for skid marks and survivors.

Child carved out of myself,
each breath stabs me a reminder
of my green girl
not yet in her season
and I the empty gourd.

I drape my life around me
like an old coat,
trace your patterns through the house
and climb the stairs until
I reach the hovering place
where I can say

My eyes were steady enough
My body shelter enough
My right arm love enough

RUTH DAIGON initially made her cultural contributions
in the field of music, rising to the role of soprano soloist
with the New York Pro Musica, making many
recordings, as well as television and concert appear-
ances. After settling in Connecticut, she began writing
poetry and has been working for the past few years on an
amalgam of music and poetry.

MEMORY OF FLESH

by Roberta Parry

Soap   wheres the soap   Lavender   Mothers soap   the last bar.

Hot waters running out again   dammit   thank god I got my hair washed   Have to call the plumber and the man for the stove   hope he can come today Ill need the extra burner   the plumber after tomorrow hell make a mess   we probably need a new tank   Call the plumber and the stove man   Run the errands   the bank cleaners drug store groceries candles placemats napkins   flowers last   on the way home   after the drug store   Get more soap   lavender   No   let it go.

Towels wet   Jack used it   dammit   he always grabs mine   take his   I should change places   Towel smells   mildewed   bathroom too damp need a vent house not worth it need a new house.

Lotion   EXTRA DRY SKIN CARE   skins so dry worse in summer   salt water chlorine suntan   age dries it out   but I love it feels so good makes me feel younger healthier   No correlation with sun the doctor said   only on the skin   but Im careful I time myself it relaxes me   A correlation with stress he said   wish summer would hurry its been a long winter.

Flesh beginning to hang from my thighs   looks old ugly Im getting old   looks like Mothers legs   her thighs were her weakest part fleshy the skin always sagged loose on her bone bad legs   mine arent as bad   All wasted away the bone cutting under the flesh the flesh all limp and draggy the muscles shriveled and slack   She couldnt stand   Here Mother put your arms around my neck rock with me   1 2 3 up thats the girl She laughed she liked it   like dancing   she loved to dance   She wouldnt let anyone else do it   she thought

73

we were good we had the timing we fit.

My hands like hers too   bigger heavier coarser hands to work peasant hands strong hands   mine bigger hers stronger   Her piano hands   she played Chopin how did she play Chopin how did she reach over an octave with those short stubby hands   Hands to pound to wrest power to wield hands to manipulate Manipulator   You manipulated everything everyone me Daddy Bonny   only we knew we saw you Everyone thought you were such a lady an angel a saint president of the church womens guild vice-president of the PTA Girl Scout leader   sympathetic ear and advisor to the lonely lost and erring   but we knew you   You destroyed us you destroyed Daddy

He was weak   you wanted more more than he could give   you pushed   Better Bob this year better we made 9 thousand and see how easy next year 12 this year 12 see how easy next year 15   15 next year 20 Ill help you you helped him you told him how you corrected him you ran him   He gave way he gave up He drank he drinks   Bankruptcy   Why didn't you let him go   you should have you shouldnt have saved him You said you had to you were saving us   you were only saving yourself   You should have let him make his own mistakes go down his own way   you would have had more left from bankruptcy   You said I didn't understand I was too young it was a matter of integrity I was sixteen I understood   it was pride   proud too proud   you wouldnt be defeated you made it a victory 50 cents on the dollar gentlemen take it or leave it sorry its the best I can offer otherwise 20   Thank you Celia They took it they took away their liens   They thought you were great didnt they you thought you were great You showed him he could be saved you showed him you could do it   he made the mess you cleaned it up after him   You could always do better you always knew more

74

you were always stronger   stronger than anyone   And
when he was broke a broken man you borrowed from the
same men and started your own business   a dress shop
a dress

      Dress what dress   I have to get it ready   the
green silk   no something long Ginny Price will wear a
long dress   my hostess gown the one with all the lace
the one Mother gave me   She had ten long dresses they
were too small I had to send them to Bonny   I better
check my shoes too   and leave the dress to be pressed
She loved clothes   beautiful clothes I always had
beautiful clothes I was the best-dressed girl in school
nylon hose   in high school   You knew that you smiled
it was your plan   out of shame out of humiliation never
poor again   Upward-bound striving good as anyone
Better   past striving you were driven   You spent   all
those clothes all those shoes and handbags and hats
two shopping trips a year one for spring and summer one
for fall and winter   All that new furniture the new cars
the mink   All those charge accounts and bills   all
those bills unpaid   Bad notices the electric power
turned off   You frightened Daddy you shamed me.

      Crazy   all those crazy things you did all that
money you borrowed all those poor people   those
people were your friends they lent to you because you
were their friend   You left them they dont have their
money its gone all gone   And you didnt tell me   you
lied   you hid it you hid from it   you couldnt face all
those people you couldnt face yourself   20 thousand
dollars   William Wendell lent you 20 thousand dollars
he wrote me I saw the cancelled checks   You could
always work men you knew how to get from them what
you wanted   Daddy broke his spirit trying to please you

    Always men   you hated men you said they couldnt be
trusted they always let you down   but you needed them
so you used them   Where is it what did you do with all

that money   How did you mismanage it   20 thousand
dollars could have financed your business for a year it
was more than enough to get you started   But you took
more thousands more   10 thousand from Daddy all his
savings all his stock   7 thousand from the Mertons 4
thousand from the Parks 2 thousand from Carolyn
Shaeffer   She called she needed the money how could
you do that   you never thought of her you never said a
word   when you called her when she came to visit
When you had the thousand gift from Arnold Jensen you
could have given it to Carolyn you could have given it to
the Parks you could have given it to Daddy   You had me
buy you more clothes clothes you never wore you sent
them home you never saw them again   I didnt know
you make me carry your shame.
        Drier   Ive got to get a new brush this doesnt
shape my hair right   something long and rounded   at
the drug store on the way home   I blow-dried her hair
with this brush she had beautiful hair so thick no gray a
beautiful color   honey   but she colored it   how
much gray under the color   It was frosted on the plane
Id never seen it frosted   like mine   only mines
sun-streaked   natural   She patted her hair   her first
gesture   The moment she saw me she touched her hair
a pathetic gesture   Am I all right   Hello Mother Youre
so beautiful   youve always been so beautiful   She was
frightened her eyes were so large cerulean blue too shiny
but she smiled   Do I look all right   You look beautiful
Mother   We carried her off she couldnt walk   the
paralysis was moving down   by the hour   the
stretcher the ambulance the siren   Just in time the
doctor said   The size of an orange   on your spine
You worked so hard you wouldnt give up   I moved your
toes I stretched your feet I exercised your legs   You
walked you used the walker   you were so proud   like a
child   you walked like a child

You wanted a cane a silver-headed ebony cane   I looked I found your silver-headed cane   but I didnt buy it for you   It was too late   you couldnt use it you couldnt use your arm   so soon it was too late   another tumor a three-inch fracture   you lost the use of your arm   As good as new the doctors said   with the steel rod   but it wasnt it hurt   You had such pain   I was frightened you were gone so long   I waited but they made me go back upstairs   You were so sick   the ether   I held your head I wiped your mouth all that putrid yellow bile   I made you blow the balloon I gave you cold compresses I held your hand your frail diminished hand   You were so happy to see me you were so glad   you didn't want to be alone you were afraid of being alone you were afraid of being left   I didnt leave you   all your life things kept leaving you so little left   You cant use people Mother you cant bend them to fit your needs   not if you want them to love you and you did   But you made things mean love you made things out of love   And in the end you had nothing all your plans went wrong   Im so sorry Mother so sorry You couldnt understand it you never understood   all the time working so hard you were working against yourself   you undid everything you ever wanted   You wouldnt let it come you couldnt accept what we had to give you had to make it   you had to have it your way And all you had left in the end were your jewels   You counted them out   so sad so terribly terribly sad Propped in your chair you doled them out   your wealth your accumulated riches from a lifetime.

My face   wheres my cream   no make-up too harsh too drying   Wrinkles   Im showing my age   is it too much tanning   but I watch   ten minutes on my face no more   She always sunbathed   every day copper brown   all year   beautiful skin so soft so smooth   satin coppery satin   she smelled so good

like cocoa butter and baby oil   And she didnt age   she
said she did I didnt see it   Ten years I didnt see her
we didnt speak for three   she didnt want to see me
She had a face job   cosmetic surgery she said face job I
said   Cosmetic surgery   Face job   she didnt like it I
had to laugh   Ill never go that way   too proud   I want
to age with dignity   Youre a good-looking woman for
your age Eva she said   I wasnt flattered I should have
been it made me sound old   Ive been dying to have the
nurses meet you she said Ive been telling them all about
you I want them to see if I described you right   How did
you describe me   I wanted to know I wanted to know
how she sees me   I told them youre not exactly a pretty
woman she said but you have style   You were pleased
you were pleased I have style at least I have style   But
you forget Mother   I was pretty very very pretty
Remember   the beauty contest football queen frater-
nity queen the county fair the modeling the award-
winning portrait   You were so proud it was what you
wanted   a pretty possession another jewel to wear it
was the way you raised me   a reflection on you your
reflection   I did it for you to make you like me   But it
wasnt enough you forgot you traded me in   for Bonny
        You named her Bonny because you thought she
was such a beautiful baby   She lived up to her name
But she only placed I won the prizes I took the blue
ribbons   You forgot I took the ribbons Mother you were
thinking of Bonny you were missing Bonny the child of
your middle age   You were going to enjoy this one you
said she wasnt going to be like me you werent going to
raise another like me   You took down all my pictures
and replaced them with larger pictures of her   Over the
piano a huge oil portrait   hundreds of dollars   You put
me away you couldnt find me anywhere in the house you
couldnt see me Id never lived there   I was gone   But I
was there Mother when you needed me   for six long

months I was there   Where was Bonny   She left you
she told me the things you did   you didnt want to share
her you took her from Daddy   he was alone all alone
you wouldnt see him   you didnt want him to see you
you made me send him away   She came for the jewelry
your child her mothers daughter   She watched you but
she wouldnt touch you   But I was there wasnt I Mother
was the one who was there   You wrote me off you didnt
want me you didnt like me   I refused to fit your mold I
resisted you I fought   but you couldnt beat me   And in
the end you loved me   you were surprised you loved me
you didnt think you did you said it   I didnt think I loved
you

   I didnt want to be like you I wasnt I learned from
you   the hard way   I would have liked to have liked
you   all we have between us is love   we salvaged that
like the Phoenix   out of the ashes out of the urn
Facing death you finally faced me facing death we finally
embraced   But Mother weve been facing death all our
lives   All my life Ive watched your face loving its beauty
wanting it to love me hating you when it didnt   I tried to
make your face my mirror   to see in it something
between us something shared a bond   a binding within
not bonds twisted cords of need rejection love and hate
holding us together tearing us apart cutting flesh as we
wrenched to and from each other   So close the
progression so easy the transition   from need to love to
rejection to hate   I needed to love you you needed love
you hated your need you rejected mine   You accepted
my life only as you relinquished your own   when you
could fight no longer you surrendered   you surrendered
to me   your strength gone to your weakness now my
strength   Yes so easy the transition so subtle the shift
I became yours as you became mine

   Yes   you are mine   You are my mother   I was
there to care for you when you needed me in need I was
there   I bathed you your bloated wasted body   I

79

creamed your face your still beautiful face the fine patrician bones beneath the fragile shell of flesh   I held your arm while you put on your lipstick and mascara you wouldnt let it go you insisted   I dressed you and brushed your wig the wig I got you   Poor Aunt Susan she brought you a hot brush   you laughed you were good to laugh to see the humor the irony   it helped Aunt Susan   You had no hair your head was bald with soft new fuzz like a baby   I smoothed the fuzz I felt the tumors I saw them grow   day by day each day bigger I never told you you never knew they were there I didnt want you to worry theyd devour your brain before the others devoured your body   All through your body all over huge swelling lumps eating away   Your body was smooth as a babys no hair no pubic hair like a baby   My baby   I carried you with my strength I fed you I changed you I slept at your bedside I sang to you I talked away your drug-laden nightmares and crawling creatures I cradled you in my arms and kissed your face Your beautiful face   Your face your face your face my god your face   I wanted it to stop I did everything to make it stop   morphine morphine more morphine 22ccs in one hour hours and hours   I couldnt make it stop the horror the ghastly silent screaming horror And when it stopped you were gone

Tell me it didn't hurt Mama tell me you didnt feel it make it go away Make your face go away.

ROBERTA PARRY of Teaneck, New Jersey writes short stories, novels, and plays. Her play ''Dreamhouse for Madness'' was a 1983 winner in the Northern Kentucky University New Play Festival, where it received full production. Prior to that, it won Columbia University's annual play-writing award. ''Memory of Flesh'' was written in eulogy to her mother, as affirmation of their relationship, which was resolved during the months her mother was dying of cancer.

THE LISTENER

by Pat Carr

I

"Hello there," she said, bracing herself against the words, hating them as she said them, despising their labored cheerfulness.

The stench of rotting flesh, waste fluids, the amassed dead white cells of pus filled her nostrils, and she automatically shallowed her breath as she walked to the side of the bed and looked down at the face so much like her own, and yet so puckered and collapsed that it was no longer like her own.

Her mother opened her eyes and smiled, but the heavy jowls of the aging disease made it into the smile of a stranger.

In her answering smile, Nicole felt the lines around her own mouth, the skin at her throat beginning to fall away from her bones the way her mother's had.

"How are we doing?" She'd given in to it herself, like the doctors and the nurses, all identifying, making the pain and the putrifying stillness of the room something they too shared.

"They tell me I'm coming along fine today." Even her mother's voice had faded into the tones of a woman decades older, and the words whispered out in exhausted puffs of air. "How was your party last night?"

She didn't want to talk about it, didn't want to spend the movement of her lips on the party, but her popularity was a source of pleasure to her mother, and since her mother had always heard about her parties, she tried to maintain that semblance of the past with, "You should have seen Laine, prancing around in chartreuse chiffon, serving that awful green cheese ball of hers that tastes like soap."

Her mother's head changed position as if she were sitting up straighter, attentive, eager, the way she'd always listened to Nicole, but the clear liquid in the tube attached to one wrist hung immobile above the bed, and the arms at the sides of the body didn't move.

"She's making such an obvious play for Jorge that I can't fathom why Gordon keeps ignoring it." Nicole looped her coat over the back of the hospital chair, sat down and watched her mother's small and perfect teeth. The two of them had been so similar, but the proliferating tumors had begun to press against one eye, popping it from the socket to make room for their own impatient spheres, and now only her mother's teeth remained the same in the melting, dragging face.

She detailed the specifics of the evening, smiled, nodded, until at last she paused and her mother said, "Have you heard anything from Phillip?"

It was a question asked every other day, one that had an identical negative answer every other day, but which she tried to alter in the timelessness of her mother's dying.

"He's going back to the Orient next month," she said this time as though both she and her mother hadn't known since the separation that Phillip would be going to Japan in January. Her mother had liked Phillip, had been very much in favor of the marriage, and she tried not to say too much against him. "I've told him I'll file as soon as he gets back," she added as though that too were fresh news. "There's no sense in his keeping that little girl circling around like a moth in his own private bottle."

She'd purposely included that to remind her mother that Phillip did have one great and glaring flaw. She'd mentioned the girl, all the girls, at one time or another to her mother, but she was never sure how much her mother cared to remember from one unaltering day to the next.

She didn't want to discuss Phillip or their marriage, but "I don't know how she's stood it this long," she went on, not wanting to go on. "I don't know how I stuck it out for as long as I did."

82

Phillip had two tattoos on his left forearm, both on the same arm, the patterns jostling each other. One was a blue eagle clutching red arrows in its talons that resembled a stalk of bananas, the other a blue scroll with a name in it. They were his single teen-aged rebellion against his father, bought one night in Juarez along with seventeen illegal beers. They'd been intended as a mark of freedom, but the fact that he had them both needled on the same muscle, as if he couldn't break out with more than one arm, had somehow made them vain and trivial, as she'd come to see everything Phillip did.

It was strange that she couldn't remember the name in the scroll. Tattooed in red ink, "And painful as hell," Phillip said, flexing the muscle, letting the two etched designs ripple together. A red name to match the red arrows in the banana talons, but she couldn't remember it.

"Well, here we are." A diminutive nurse came briskly in, balancing a tray with plastic glass of orange juice and tiny paper nut cup of pills. Her white hand, that was still plump enough to have dimples across the knuckles, shook down the scarlet mercury, laid a thermometer beneath her mother's swollen tongue.

Every day the same irrelevancy, the same needless measurement of how much life was left.

Nicole looked away from the white starched little nurse with her white starched cap, glanced around the room.

It was filthy.

Dust lay on the chrome tongues of the bedside table drawers, on the iron struts of the bed. The bottle of motionless liquid was crystally sterile, but the metal foot of the stand that supported it was furred with bandage lint. The wastebasket foamed with used gauze pads, and yesterday's plastic glasses on the dresser were stacked four deep.

She knew it was only natural that they had to be less concerned with the terminal, that they had to save their bright bird words for those less badly dying, but the

83

oversights of neglect were too visible, too painful.

"There now, that wasn't so unpleasant, was it?"

She brought her gaze back from the floor litter to the nurse.

Why were they always blond? Even in El Paso, always petite and blond and would have smelled of coconut lotion if the hospital odors hadn't been so strong, and always used words like "pleasant" for hospital rituals.

That was a word she'd heard all her life. A word her mother had used for her since elementary school, talking about her or to her, saying, "She's (or You're) such a pleasant little person, it's no wonder so many people want to be around her (or you)." "You're always so pleasant and calm," her friends added. "You never seem to have any problems, and you're always ready to hear other people's. How can anyone listen as well as you do?" they marvelled. "How can anyone be so damned polite?" Phillip had shouted.

Of course she knew how, but she didn't try to explain. She had her mother who listened, and whose listening had created a duty, a *noblesse oblige*, for her to listen in turn to the others who didn't have such an avid audience. It was something that came with the politeness her mother had instilled in her, knowing she had to hear them out the way she knew never to take just one grape from a bunch that would leave the raw and ugly stem for the next person served. She'd known since childhood that having a perfect listener of her own gave her the obligation to listen to the rest.

The nurse's dimpled hand jotted neat numerical results of the temperature and pulse count. "Now don't forget your pills this time." She flicked starchily out the door.

As she disappeared, an ancient cough of a laugh, a terrible parody of her mother's once rich chuckle, came from the bed. "What good are they anyway? I didn't bother to take them yesterday."

It didn't matter. Nothing the hospital staff did,

could do, would matter to the multiplying tumors.
with its plastic liner, and they disappeared beneath the bulge of dried purulent gauzes.

"But I suppose I could try them today."

The orange juice had already separated into two discernible ribbons of pale and darker gold, and Nicole mixed it with the straw. "I can throw them away if you'd rather."

The good eye studied her face.

"All right."

She brought the juice to the bed, touched the straw to her mother's tongue that was the white of powdered adobe brick. Then she slid the pills into the woven basket

II

She laid her gloves on the table, pushed her coat back from her shoulders onto the lounge chair. She didn't want to wait there, didn't want a cocktail or a conversation with Laine, but then she couldn't remember when she'd last been somewhere she'd actually wanted to be. Perhaps this one time she could beg off, write a note of apology, leave be. . .

But she saw Laine peering near-sightedly into the lounge, and she affixed her pleasant smile.

"Hi."

Nicole maintained the smile.

"You think it's going to be cold out since it was snowing this morning, but sheesh, does it get hot. You've got to see what I bought. What're you having to drink?"

Nicole watched her pull off the olive leather coat, the matching gloves that she knew Gordon had picked out. "Scotch and soda."

"O-o-o-o. I don't know how you can stand those awful things. Look. Isn't this cute?" She'd pulled out a black silk bikini, a top that was nothing more than a black silk ribbon with straps and dangling fringe. "I have to have something that tastes good or I can't drink at all."

"Hm-mn-m-m," Nicole said toward the black silk

pieces as Laine stuffed them back into their lettered white paper sacks.

"Wait till I tell you. . ."

The waitress swayed near them. "You ready to order?" She had the faintest trace of a Spanish accent, and the roots of her lemon hair were black.

"A Scotch and soda."

"How about a *piña colada*? Are they good?"

The girl nodded. "We sell a lot of them."

"Does that sound good, Nikki?"

"They're awfully sweet."

"You know I'm a chocolate junky. Gordon says that the sign of a potential alcoholic is that they eat tons of chocolate. Okay. One of them." Then she eased back in the chair, looked at Nicole. "I don't know how you do it. You're always so. . .so polished, so pleasant. You're always so serene." Then she seemed to remember. "Oh, how's your mother?"

Nicole shrugged. "As well as those things go." She'd practiced the tone, the even answer, and the desire to tell Laine, or anyone, how her mother really was didn't surface. "You know how it is."

She was sure Laine didn't know how it was, but the equated experience was something everyone took for granted.

And Laine nodded. "Hospitals are so depressing."

"They do such indignity to the human soul." It was a gratuitous slice of truth that Laine could carry away with her like the packages at her feet.

Laine's eyes registered the information and the compliment to her perception, but Nicole recognized that she was engrossed in something else. "You'll just die when you hear, Nikki." Her voice was ringingly clear in its self-absorption. "You remember Jorge and I went to a concert in Las Cruces last week?"

Nicole nodded, not remembering, not needing to have remembered.

"Well. . .while we were there and Gordon was on one of his trips to Dallas, we just took some extra time and stopped off at a motel."

Nicole took a sip of the cold Scotch as Laine leaned into her story as if it were an experience Nicole had never heard.

Why did they all think their own affair was so singularly unique? Why did they all think they were the only ones who talked to her? She could feel the capillaries around her lips radiating into aging creases.

"That's the first step toward divorce," she said gently. "I ought to know."

Laine's immediate attention parted her lips. "Did you have an affair on Phillip? That gorgeous hunk?"

"A long time ago." Over a thousand years before. Her own futile attempt at striking back, an attempt as abortive as Phillip's tattoos. She regretted her moment of candor. "It's too old to remember very well."

Laine was studying her with delight. "I didn't know that. A Latin lover like Jorge?"

"Not exactly." The impulse to warn Laine had evaporated.

"You know, Nikki, you really do seem to know everything. You're the one person I feel I can really talk to. You're the only person who I can tell. . ."

She didn't want to hear it. To sit and smile through yet another confession was more than she could stand. Her arms seemed to itch from inside, from near the bone. She opened her purse quickly, signalled the waitress. "I've got to go. A dinner party tonight that. . . Here. Let me get these."

She forced herself to keep smiling as she carefully wrote in the tip, signed the tab. She'd make it up to Laine later, listen more closely, more extendedly, the next time.

As she dropped the pen back in her purse, she saw the hurt and interrupted expression on Laine's face. "I'll give you a ring," she said and stood up.

She let herself in, shut the heavy door, and called out, "*Magdalena, yo estoy.*" She paused at the stucco arch of the Victorian living room. The sky and the earth had turned the metallic gray of pewter, and the twilight edges of the room made her restless, depressed.

She stood for a moment, then shrugged off the coat as she went down the hall to the bedroom she'd occupied since her return.

Why had she accepted a dinner invitation?

She dropped the coat on the bed and opened the closet.

The switch on the ancient wall didn't work, and she reached her fingers toward the lightbulb, having to force her every movement.

A dinner invitation. An extended meal at which she would have to listen pleasantly, swallow course after course besides the words that others would tell her.

Her fingers twisted the globe, and the sudden brilliance made her pupils contract with pain, made patches of intense yellow dance across the hangers of clothes.

So many clothes. Row upon row. Boxes of jewelry, boxes and boxes of expensive clothes, all of the items Phillip had bought for his attempted atonement.

Perhaps a sweater and skirt.

She pulled out the built-in drawer and focused on the sweaters.

They were in subdued shades of gray, tan, oatmeal. The quiet hues that Phillip insisted were the only possible ones for the wardrobe of any woman who was truly a lady.

But of course his definition of a lady embraced a pedestalled, well-groomed female who wasn't fond of sex and who thus allowed gratification elsewhere. The grays, fawns, beiges were the subdued and frightened shades of Phillip's own imagination.

She lifted the careful pile of wool and extracted a

sweater from below, a deep wine-colored sweater her mother had given her one long-before Christmas.

There would be no more gifts from her mother.

She held it in her hands and looked down at it.

The deep rich wine of the sweater was suddenly every present, every surprise from her mother. There in the dark red yarn were all the childhood Valentine parties, all the garnet birthdays, all the adult cherry-papered gifts. If she could only wrap the lustrous sweater in tissue paper, keep it for another score of ruby Christmases. . .

She could see the back of her hand around the scarlet weave and she felt the veins through the skin that was like her mother's.

Already her hands had begun to age. "Good rings will call attention to themselves, not your hands," Phillip had said calmly, choosing another smoky topaz in the chestnut shade he'd have worn himself if the fashion for men had allowed it.

"*Señora?*"

Magdalena's voice came from the kitchen.

"*Sí?*"

"*El hospital, señora. El telefono. . .Su madre. . .*"

IV

As she went in the hospital room her mother gave her a tired, polite smile before she closed her unaffected eye again.

No one could really understand about the politeness or the pleasantness, about the dying with polite and careful regard for the person who would stay behind.

She wanted to touch her mother, press the glass thinness of the bone hands, but she didn't. She merely dragged the chair close to the side of the bed and sat down.

Her mother was beginning to breathe with difficulty.

She sat very still beside the bed. "Don't go. Don't

leave me yet," rose to her mouth, but she didn't say it. It would have interrupted her mother's reserve, would have shocked her mother to hear it.

The room, the hospital, were silent.

Then her mother opened the normal eye very wide once more and a fevered glint glowed in it. She raised her head away from the pillow and looked into Nicole's face. The golden brown of her iris shown as if back-lighted, as if reflecting a copper mirror.

It was a glitter of knowledge, a glow of satisfaction.

And Nicole knew as she stared into her mother's eye that her mother was aware that she was dying. And the eye acknowledged that Nicole knew as well, and it was fiercely pleased in the way people are strangely, morbidly, pleased to be the bearers of disaster news.

Their glances held, and then the good eye closed and her mother's head dropped back onto the pillow.

Nicole reached out and pressed the emergency call button hard.

An immediate step squeaked on the tile floor as if someone had been waiting for the buzzer, and she partially felt, partially saw someone come in, go out again. She didn't look away from her mother's face in its ancient final stage.

The crepe soled shoes returned, and there were two sets of them dragging a tank of oxygen. "Excuse me," one of the nurse voices said, and Nicole got up, moved to the curved metal end of the bed.

They put a tiny green mask over her mother's nose and mouth, and one of them turned the handle of the little tank.

Her mother didn't open her eye, didn't alter the wet choked timbre of her breathing.

"She's going," one of them said, and the other one nodded, turned the knob of the tank. Neither of them acknowledged Nicole.

She noticed that the one working the tank was wearing thick red lipstick, greasy and heavily layered, vitreous in the hospital light.

The other nurse shoved aside the chair, the clear liquid that had hung so long above the bed and her mother.

No. Not her mother any longer, a figure on a white hospital bed with a green triangular plastic cup over its face, a figure with pale yellow fingers that rustled, clutched at the nubbed bedspread.

The nurse fiddled busily with the dial, and the white nurse cloth rasped in the dead air.

Then the green plastic diaphragm sucked into the mouth, stayed tight against the nostrils, lips.

"She's gone," one of the nurse voices said very softly.

Yet still the hands moved, the fingers curving into claws that flexed, pulled into the palms, slowed, extended once more.

"We can. . .," one of the nurses began, but as they looked at Nicole the words quit abruptly.

She didn't know what they'd seen in her face, but she didn't say anything.

Both the eyes were half open, the blue-whites of the corneas showing empty, gleaming like an edge of rinsed porcelain beneath the lids.

In the winter evening outside, cars were accelerating, stopping, a bus at the corner was coughing exhaust, and inside the hospital, trays and metal dishes were being distributed down the hall. Her mother's order would be on the cart, on an individual aluminum dinner tray ready to be delivered.

V

The entryway, the steps, were the same, the knocker as loud, clacking against itself, as she opened the unaltered door.

Magdalena stood just inside, her massive body encased in blue nylon, her bloated hands unstrung at her sides.

91

"*Su madre, esta. . .?*"

"*Esta muerta.*"

Magdalena clapped one mountainous brown hand across her mouth. "*Lo siento, lo siento,*" she said through the fingers.

"*Gracias.*" It was all so formal, so distant in Spanish, the allotted words for "I'm sorry" from another time and place.

"*Gracias,*" Nicole said again and turned away.

The living room was cold, but Magdalena had turned on the lamps, and the polished tops of the tables echoed them silently.

There was no one now for her to talk to. For the first time in her life, she had no one to tell anything to. There was no one to whom she could relate her triumphs, to whom she could recount her simple comings and goings.

A phone rang back in the house, and she was conscious that Magdalena's bulk had pulled away from the stucco archway.

She was isolated. Completely and voicelessly alone. There was no one left to listen to her.

She moved toward the living room window.

Magdalena's heavy steps were coming back from the kitchen to the front of the house. "*Por usted, señora.*"

But now she herself never again had to listen to others. She nodded to register Magdalena's presence, but she didn't turn from the window. "*Yo no estoy, Magdalena.*"

"*Cómo?*"

Nicole pulled aside one of the thick satin drapes and looked through the glass into the desert night. "Tell whoever it is that I'm not home."

There was a lengthy pause, and then Magdalena said at last, "*Sí, señora.*"

The mountain was a gathered darkness like a black cloud bank. Against the darkness, a bush was caught in the two dimensional glare of a street lamp, its scarlet winter leaves suspended like drying blood in the act of clotting brown.

She leaned her forehead against the cold glass that contained the night. She felt a constriction start in the back of her throat, felt a liquification begin without effort, without volition, deep inside the black and silent caverns of her skull.

PAT CARR was born in 1932 in Grass Creek, Wyoming and holds a Ph.D. in English from Tulane. She has published five books, including *The Grass Creek Chronicle* (1976) and *The Women in the Mirror* (1977) which won the Iowa School of Letters Short Fiction Award for 1977. Her short stories have been published in such literary journals as *Southern Review, Yale Review* and in *Best American Short Stories*. She is currently living at the edge of the Ozarks with her writer husband and writing full time.

continuity

POEM FOR MOTHER'S DAY

by Serena Fusek

I

I should have been
aborted.
My mother was a beautiful
girl who didn't need
the responsibility
and competition
of a baby girl
to age her.

My mother
should have been
aborted.
She was an only child
an accident who happened
to a woman surprised
only once by passion.

Two generations of women
who didn't want to give
life.

The third generation
dreams of death
as a handsome lover.

I cannot imagine new life
started inside me.
The death I should have died
in the womb of a mother
who should not have been born
has rotted out
all my soft parts
and left only bones.
There is no place for a baby
to nestle.
If she were born
Death
would be her twin.

SERENA FUSEK has been writing almost since she
could read. Before then she made up stories aloud. Her
education after high school has derived from travel,
museums, the public library, some college courses and
living. After spending two years in Europe, she and her
husband settled in Tidewater, Virginia where she
remains, by choice, childless.

THE MADONNA CYCLE

by Joyce S. Mettleman

I

My mourning for you has begun before the fact itself.
I speak to you, hear the thin pipings of your voice;
Respond, say things to make you laugh —
And even laugh myself.
But I know the time is near.
My instinct, prescience, call it what-you-will
Sends messages I cannot ignore.
I shiver.
Hairs at the back of my neck stand up.
Alarmed, fearful — fight or run?
Neither, this time —
Fight tears; run my show,
Try to keep you from pain —
I cannot keep you from death,
That final, fatal fact of life.
I mourn so many things:
That pain has partially erased the mother-you;
That we could not be close
In ways that we could not be close;
That we'll no longer be close in ways that we were close;
That you were born when you were
And burdened with constraints that kept you so
    confined.
That this is being written for myself:
That you will never see or understand.

II

Which is the more difficult role — parent or child?
I say it's being the child,
For it refers to a past almost forgotten,
A time of dependence,
An age through which, hopefully, one has grown.
Unless a new rapport has been forged
And the parent has signaled,

Consciously recognized the emergence of a mature personality,
One is forever a child;
Always seen through parental eyes,
Doomed to infinite childhood.
To all parents, we are children.
To some who have taken that next step of awareness and recognition,
We are — finally — people.

III

Curled in the depths of my blue-velvet sofa,
Soothed in its womb-like silkiness,
I am struck by — motherhood.
Is that the word?
I mean the dailiness of being a mother:
That complex interweaving of tugs and pulls on the heart;
Emotional floods, quick storms,
Sudden wonder at each child's deliverance and perfection.
And then that mirror reversal:
Memories of being mothered, held, advised, punished,
Colored now by the perspective of years;
Words and acts understood now, accepted and even forgiven.
I see the line of progression:
Mother, daughter become mother; then daughter.
From rosy child skipping across smooth slates,
Sharing a kettle's weight of warm soup between us,
After visiting her mother on a red-gold September day;
To teen-age daughter,
Finding solace in the crisp white linens and shining candles of the Sabbath meal;
To weary, diaper-obsessed mother

Trying, through years of touching, withdrawal, talking,
    silences,
Misunderstandings and closeness
To reach her own daughter.
Now she journeys once again
To see the final person her mother has become.
Never really close through her adolescence,
They are that now, for she understands, accepts,
    forgives
And — best of all — loves.
She feels all the vibrating connections,
Sends thoughts out to her own children,
Goes forward, arms outstretched,
Knowing that time need not restrict:
Mothers are daughters, daughters are mothers.
We link arms and stand together.

JOYCE S. METTELMAN was born and has lived all her
life in upstate New York. Graduated from Vassar College
in 1952 with a B.A. in English, she is a writer who has
also worked as homemaker and mother, public relations
person, service volunteer and developmental researcher
at Hamilton College. Primarily a poet, she has also
completed a novel — unpublished so far. She and her
husband, Dr. Arthur Mettelman, have three grown
children.

THE UNBROKEN CIRCLE

by *Alana Harris-Rohr*

We rock and sway together,
Never missing a beat.
Feelings exposed, glittering, and tender.
Only with you can I give
So unabashedly,
So freely.
Perhaps I have always connected love
With innocence,
And I see so much innocence
Hiding behind those spidery lashes,
So much naivete
Floating in your sea blue eyes.
You are as much a part of me now
As when you were nestled in my womb.
A tiny mermaid blowing bubbles
Into warm, dark waters.
Your breath is still my breath,
And your blood flows like a red tide
In my veins,
For when you hurt,
I bleed.
It has always been that way
From time immemorial.
A mother-daughter bond as old as the universe.
A line of undying devotion
That will flow throughout the ages
Long after we both are gone.
I watch you sleep,
Dreams curled like silver pebbles in your tiny fists,
And I am bathed in the pureness of your beauty.
Someday you will hold in your arms a new universe.
You will scan the same untouched horizons,
Pulses quickening as mine do now.
You will gaze into your daughter's eyes,
And you will be as touched by her as I was by you
These many, long years before.

Thus, the tradition will continue.
From grandmother to mother to daughter to grand-
daughter,
And to every generation of women to come —
An unbroken circle of motherly love.

ALANA HARRIS-ROHR has been writing poetry and
short stories for the last 20 years. She has also written
and illustrated a children's book called *The Magic
Swing*. "The Unbroken Circle" was created to celebrate
that invisible line of loving energy that flowed from her
mother, increasing in intensity when her daughter
Brenna was born.

Vintage'45 Press

Vintage '45 Press also publishes *Vintage '45*, a uniquely supportive quarterly journal for women. For further information on this magazine or to reorder copies of *Maternal Legacy* please write to Vintage '45 Press, P. O. Box 266, Orinda, CA 94563-0266.